DeWitt and Lila

Wallace

TWENTY CENTS

DECEMBER 10, 1951

TIME

THE WEEKLY NEWSMAGAZINE

Boris Chaliapin

THE DeWITT WALLACES
With scissors, paste and sunrises, 15,500,000 customers.

$6.00 A YEAR   (REG. U.S. PAT. OFF.)   VOL. LVIII NO. 24

DeWitt and Lila Wallace

Community Builders

Charity for All

by Brendan January

Children's Press®
A Division of Grolier Publishing
New York London Hong Kong Sydney
Danbury, Connecticut

Photo Credits

Photographs ©: 1951 Time Inc.: 2; AP/Wide World Photos: 43; Archive Photos: 11, 29; Boys & Girls Clubs of America: 44; Christine Osinski: 48; Macalester College: cover, 7, 22, 36; The Metropolitan Museum of Art: 39, 41 (James Selkin); Minnesota Historical Society: 19, 20, 8, 12 (C.P. Gibson); New York Public Library Picture Collection: 33; Outward Bound USA: 37; Reader's Digest Association: 23; Roy Stevens: 26, 30, 32, 35; Tony Stone Images: 45 (Frank Siteman); U.N.O. Division of Special Collections & University Archives: 14, 15; UPI/Corbis-Bettmann: 3, 9, 16, 25, 42; Y.W.C.A of the U.S.A. National Board Archives: 18.

Reading Consultant
Linda Cornwell, Learning Resource Consultant
Indiana Department of Education

Visit Children's Press on the Internet at:
http://publishing.grolier.com

Library of Congress Cataloging-in-Publication Data

January, Brendan, 1972-
    DeWitt and Lila Wallace : charity for all / by Brendan January.
       p. cm. — (Community builders)
    Includes biographical references and index.
    Summary: A biography of DeWitt and Lila Wallace, founders of "Reader's Digest" and philanthropists who donated the majority of their vast fortune to worthy causes.
    ISBN: 0-516-20843-8 (lib. bdg.)   0-516-26329-3 (pbk.)
    1. Reader's digest. 2. Wallace, DeWitt, 1889-1981—Juvenile literature. 3. Wallace, Lila Acheson, 1887-1984—Juvenile literature. 4. Publishers and publishing—United States—Biography—Juvenile literature. [1. Wallace, DeWitt, 1889-1981. 2. Wallace, Lila Acheson, 1887-1984. 3. Publishers and publishing. 4. Philanthropists. 5. Reader's digest.] I. Title. II. Series.
PN4900.R3B74 1998
070.5'092273—dc21
[B]   97-14997
                                                  CIP
                                                  AC

Contents

Chapter ONE

DeWitt Wallace

When DeWitt Wallace was born on November 12, 1889, his mother was delighted. He is "a prize," she wrote. DeWitt's father, however, was not impressed. "The child is a rascal . . . without character," he said. DeWitt's mother and father disagreed over the child's name. Four weeks passed before they decided to name him William Roy DeWitt Wallace. In elementary school, he preferred the name "DeWitt."

DeWitt spent his childhood in a town just outside of St. Paul, Minnesota. His father taught Greek at

Macalester College, a small school just a few blocks from DeWitt's home. As DeWitt grew up, the college took much of his father's attention. The small school didn't have much money. DeWitt's father spent most of his time on trips to raise funds for the school.

DeWitt Wallace

As DeWitt grew older, his mother became ill. The Wallace family wasn't rich, so DeWitt worked at odd jobs to help out. He was eight years old when he entered elementary school in 1897. DeWitt quickly proved to be a bright student. But he soon became more interested in clowning around than in classwork. As a result, he never completed four years of study in the same college.

During the summer of 1912, DeWitt worked as a clerk at the Webb Publishing Company in St. Paul.

**The Webb Publishing Company was located
on the third floor of this building.**

One of his jobs was to read through reports about farming. Most of these reports were several hundred pages long! They discussed new discoveries about raising crops and livestock, such as horses, sheep, and cows. Although the reports were long and boring, DeWitt learned many interesting facts. But, DeWitt wondered, how could a farmer read through so many pages to find just one or two useful pieces of information? DeWitt had an idea. Why not take the most useful information and print it in a separate magazine?

In 1915, DeWitt tried his idea. He called it *Getting the Most Out of Farming* and printed 100,000 copies. Throughout 1916, DeWitt drove around the United States, selling his little magazine in small stores and to farmers. As DeWitt traveled, he spoke to a lot of different people. At that time, many Americans

In the early 1900s, the lack of modern machinery made farming more difficult and time consuming than it is today.

lived on small farms. There was no television or radio. Newspapers were hard to find outside of large cities. DeWitt discovered that people wanted to learn more about the rest of the world. He noted in his diary: "Among these people there is a strong desire for knowledge."

DeWitt began to dream of a new idea. Instead of collecting just farming articles, why not collect many different kinds of articles? There were thousands of magazines published every month. DeWitt decided to select the most interesting and helpful articles. He would then reprint them together as a monthly magazine. Although he didn't know it at the time, DeWitt had stumbled upon one of the most successful publishing ideas in history. Eagerly, DeWitt planned his magazine's first issue.

DeWitt had to put aside his plans, however, in 1917. Since 1914, the countries of Europe had been at war. The United States tried to keep out of the fight. But in 1917, the United States declared war on Germany. DeWitt volunteered to serve in the U.S. Army. After several months of training, he was

American soldiers prepare for their departure
to Europe to fight in World War I.

sent to France. DeWitt fought bravely until he was
badly wounded, and he spent the rest of the war in
a hospital. But in all that time, DeWitt didn't forget
his dream of publishing a monthly magazine.

When the war ended in 1918, DeWitt returned to
St. Paul, Minnesota. He went straight to the library
and read through every available magazine. He
selected interesting or important articles. Then he

There were several publishing companies in St. Paul, Minnesota, in the 1920s. None was interested in DeWitt's magazine.

carefully cut out words and sentences to make the articles shorter and less confusing. Within six months, DeWitt finished his first issue. He called it *Reader's Digest.*

In January 1920, DeWitt sent an issue of *Reader's Digest* to several publishing companies. He hoped one of them would be interested in publishing it. Instead, they didn't like it at all. The pub-

Fiction and Nonfiction

Books and magazines contain two kinds of writing: fiction and nonfiction. Fictional stories are about people or events that are not real. Nonfiction stories are about real people or events that actually happened. This book is nonfiction.

lishers wondered why the magazine didn't print fiction. One publisher told DeWitt, "Your publication might reach 300,000 [people]. That's [not enough readers] for us."

DeWitt was disappointed that the publishers didn't like his idea. At age thirty-one, he didn't have a career or a wife. He felt like a failure. One night, DeWitt was having dinner with a friend. They talked about a young woman DeWitt had met four years earlier. Her name was Lila Acheson. DeWitt remembered her beauty and friendliness. He made a bold decision. DeWitt sent Lila a telegram and invited her to visit him in St. Paul.

Chapter TWO

Lila Acheson

Lila Acheson was born in Canada and grew up in the United States.

Lila Bell Acheson was born on Christmas Day, 1887. Her parents believed that she would grow up to do great things. Lila's first three years were spent on the flat farmlands of Manitoba, a province in Canada. In 1891, her father became a minister, and the family moved to North Dakota. It was the first of several moves. During the next fifteen years, Lila's family never stayed in one place for very long. She also lived in Illinois, Minnesota, and Washington State.

When Lila was eighteen, she attended college in Nashville, Tennessee. Two years later she left Nashville to attend the School of Social Services at the University of Oregon. She planned to become a social worker. Social workers try to help people solve problems that are caused by poverty, crime, illness, and unemployment. At the time, Lila was engaged to a wealthy young man from Seattle, Washington. Lila's father wanted her to get married. He didn't want her to have a career.

The University of Oregon campus about 1907, the year Lila enrolled in the School of Social Services

During World War I, women took men's places working in factories. These women are assembling airplanes to be used in the fighting.

Lila had other ideas, though. She broke the engagement and began working for the Young Women's Christian Association (YWCA). When the United States entered World War I in 1917, the YWCA asked Lila to supervise factory conditions in New Jersey. With most men fighting in Europe, millions of women began working in factories. But the working conditions were terrible. The factories were hot and crowded. The work was difficult and dangerous. Many of the women suffered serious injuries. The United States military, however, needed these workers to make uniforms, guns, and ammunition. Lila's job was to improve the working conditions for the women and to keep the factories running.

Lila's first goal was to provide the women with good, nutritious meals. She ordered crates of hot food and cold refreshments. She also decided that

The YWCA

The Young Women's Christian Association (YWCA) was founded in England in 1855. It began in the United States in 1858. The purpose of the YWCA is to improve the lives of young women throughout the world.

Factory work was difficult and sometimes boring. Lila encouraged women workers to attend social events, such as this picnic, to entertain them.

music should be played to keep the workers alert and cheerful. To fight boredom among the women, she organized local dances and other social events. Soon, there were no more accidents, and the factories ran smoothly.

After the war, Lila traveled to factories all around the country. She worked to end the diseases and filthy conditions that workers faced. By the time Lila turned thirty-two, she began to think about getting married. But she didn't want to stop working. Then Lila received DeWitt Wallace's telegram. She accepted his invitation and went to St. Paul.

On October 14, 1920, DeWitt met Lila outside her hotel. They spent the entire day together. Finally it grew dark, and DeWitt walked Lila back to her hotel. As she went inside, he said: "You are the most wonderful girl in the world. If I ask you to marry me, will you say yes?"

St. Paul, Minnesota, in 1920—as it looked when Lila visited DeWitt

DeWitt and Lila soon after their marriage, which took place on October 15, 1921

She laughed. "Don't ask me tonight. Tonight is too soon. Ask me tomorrow."

They met again the next day. DeWitt shared his dream for a new magazine called *Reader's Digest* with Lila. "What do you think?" he asked.

"It makes such perfect sense," she responded. "It cannot fail."

Lila and DeWitt were a perfect match. He asked her again to marry him. This time she said yes.

Early in 1921, DeWitt took an office job in Pittsburgh, Pennsylvania. Lila continued to work in New York City. DeWitt planned to earn some money before settling with Lila in Pittsburgh and starting the magazine. But the office routine bored DeWitt. It wasn't long before he was fired. He called Lila in New York and told her the bad news. He thought she should reconsider marrying him. But Lila replied: "This is the best thing that could happen! Now you have no more excuses. Let's get on with it [starting the magazine]!"

DeWitt worked all through the summer of 1921. He wrote lists of people he thought would be interested in his magazine. He sent letters asking professors, church groups, and women's organizations to subscribe. Lila believed that the magazine would be especially useful to women. She told DeWitt: "The war has changed everything. Women are out of their homes for the first time, working, growing, curious about the world. They can even vote!"

The Nineteenth Amendment

For a long time, women in this country were not allowed to vote. In 1920, an amendment, or change, was added to the U.S. Constitution. The amendment gave all women the right to vote.

Lila worked tirelessly reviewing manuscripts and articles that she believed should be included in *Reader's Digest*.

In January 1922, DeWitt, Lila, and several loyal workers worked through the night to wrap and address five thousand copies of their first issue of *Reader's Digest*. The next morning, exhausted and dirty, they dragged bags filled with the magazine to the local post office. From there, the five thousand issues were sent to the first customers. *Reader's Digest* was born.

Chapter THREE

The Dream is Real

THE READER'S DIGEST

THIRTY-ONE ARTICLES EACH MONTH FROM LEADING MAGAZINES — EACH ARTICLE OF ENDURING VALUE AND INTEREST, IN CONDENSED AND COMPACT FORM

FEBRUARY 1922

The February 1922 issue of *Reader's Digest* was the first issue mailed to paid subscribers.

The first issues of *Reader's Digest* looked nothing like the magazine looks today. There were no pictures and no advertisements. The magazine didn't print fiction. *Reader's Digest* was sixty-four pages long and had thirty-one articles. DeWitt's plan was for a person to read one article each day of the month before receiving the next issue. The purpose of the magazine was to educate, not to entertain. DeWitt also hoped to inspire people. *Reader's Digest* contained cheerful articles that encouraged self-help and responsibility. Upbeat stories of ordinary people's courage and success filled the magazine. But would anyone buy it?

DeWitt waited nervously for more subscriptions to arrive. All of his money was invested in the magazine. Lila continued to work in New York City, supporting them both. DeWitt spent his days in the New York Public Library, searching for articles to

The Roaring Twenties

Change was sweeping the United States during the 1920s. Movies, automobiles, and radios were becoming popular. People wanted to understand these new developments. *Reader's Digest* provided them with useful and helpful articles.

The research and reading room of the New York Public Library, where DeWitt spent much of his time looking for articles to include in *Reader's Digest*

reprint. In the evenings, Lila and DeWitt returned to their apartment and worked on future issues.

Soon, more and more people were signing up to receive Reader's Digest. Lila began to look for a new place to make the magazine. She decided that New

York City was too busy and too crowded to get much work done. One weekend she took a train to a sleepy town called Pleasantville, located 40 miles (64 kilometers) north of the city. With a population of about four thousand people, tree-lined streets, and a peaceful atmosphere, Pleasantville was indeed a pleasant town. To Lila, it was the perfect place to settle down.

Lila and DeWitt moved into a small apartment above a garage in July 1922. DeWitt moved the magazine business into the garage. Soon they felt right at home.

DeWitt and Lila's apartment was located above this garage.

Pleasantville, New York

Although *Reader's Digest* moved out of Pleasantville in the 1930s, Lila and DeWitt decided to keep the Pleasantville address. They believed that the small town had all of the morals and values their readers looked for in the magazine.

Success

For the next five years, *Reader's Digest* grew steadily. By 1925, there were more than 15,000 readers. DeWitt rented buildings in downtown Pleasantville to make room for their growing business. In 1926, there were about 30,000 readers. Just one year later, the number of readers grew to more than 60,000! By 1930, *Reader's Digest* reached 290,000 homes. The Wallaces were earning $900,000 a year.

DeWitt and Lila were astonished. They never dreamed that their magazine would be so successful. The money kept pouring in. Even while the rest of the nation was suffering in a severe depression, more and more people subscribed to *Reader's Digest* each year.

28

The Great Depression

During the 1930s, the United States was struck by a terrible depression. Many businesses and banks had to close. Millions of workers lost their jobs. In this difficult time, people turned to *Reader's Digest* for comfort and for hope.

During the Depression, people who were out of work often waited in breadlines for free meals of soup or bread.

Construction of the new *Reader's Digest* headquarters, located 7 miles (11 kilometers) north of Pleasantville, began in 1937.

Soon the "little" magazine had outgrown its home in Pleasantville. DeWitt and Lila employed hundreds of people. Every spare office space in town was used for *Reader's Digest* business. DeWitt and Lila decided to build a new headquarters.

Lila found another perfect spot in the rolling farmland just a few miles north of Pleasantville. Lila remembered how horrible working conditions could be. She was determined to create a beautiful workplace that employees could enjoy. She ordered the architects (people who design buildings) to construct a building that blended in with the surroundings, the way some mansions and college campuses do.

The architects created an elegant, three-story brick building. They placed a white tower on the roof that provided beautiful views of the countryside. The building was only part of Lila's plan. She also hired gardeners to plant hundreds of trees, create walkways, and install fountains. Thousands of flowers blossomed in the spring, surrounding the headquarters with color and fragrance.

The completed headquarters included a 32-foot-
(10-meter) high white tower on the roof.

Lila knew that most people couldn't afford to buy priceless antiques and paintings, so she shared hers with the workers.

Inside the building, the offices were furnished with fancy wood paneling and beautiful desks and chairs. Lila added a magnificent touch of her own to the decorating. For years, she had been buying outstanding works of European and American art. Lila also collected rare antiques from all over the world. But instead of keeping these items in her own home, she decided to place them in the new headquarters. "Art is not for the few. Art belongs to everyone," she said. Employees were astonished to find beautiful paintings worth millions of dollars hanging in their offices.

"We're Going to Give It Away!"

Chapter FIVE

By the end of World War II in 1945, *Reader's Digest* had become the most popular magazine in U.S. history. Its cheerful articles and positive descriptions of America attracted readers throughout the world. The Wallaces were among the richest people in the United States. But they had an unexpected problem. What would they do with all their money? DeWitt and Lila had no children. They

34

already lived in a huge house and owned the best things money could buy. So they decided to give their money away.

DeWitt had a deep desire to educate and encourage people to do their best. He often said that his company's goal was to serve people—not to make a profit. DeWitt shared the success of *Reader's Digest* with his employees by paying them generous salaries.

DeWitt and Lila's home, High Winds, had twenty-two rooms, a lookout tower, and an indoor garden.

The DeWitt Wallace Library at Macalester College
honors DeWitt's generosity.

DeWitt wanted to help others, too. He donated large sums of money to education. Macalester College, where his father had worked so hard, received millions of dollars. DeWitt also supported thousands of scholarships that helped young people to pursue their dreams.

One day in 1969, a young man named Josh Miner spoke with DeWitt. Miner was the president of the Outward Bound program in the United States.

Today, Outward Bound programs continue to teach young people to believe in their own abilities.

Outward Bound was established to build leadership and self-confidence in young people through tough camping experiences. The program started in Scotland and was a great success. Miner was eager to make the program successful in the United States. But, Miner explained to DeWitt, the program needed money. DeWitt was impressed with Josh Miner and Outward Bound. He gave Miner a small envelope and said, "I think Outward Bound is doing a splendid job and I hope this helps to keep it alive."

When Miner returned to his hotel, he opened the envelope and could hardly believe his eyes. The check inside was for $1 million! For the next several years, DeWitt continued to support Outward Bound and to help it be successful in the United States.

While DeWitt gave money to education and youth programs, Lila had projects of her own. One day in New York City, she passed the long, gray building that contains one of the greatest collections of art in the world—The Metropolitan Museum of Art. She complained about the steep stairs leading up to the

The Metropolitan Museum of Art in New York City
is famous throughout the world. Thousands of visitors
tour the museum each year.

"Art is Not For the Few"

Lila believed that everyone should have a chance to experience music, literature, dance, and art. Often, only people who live in or near big cities can attend these kinds of events. Lila remembered how alone she felt growing up in small farm towns in the Midwest. In 1967, she donated $1 million to the Metropolitan Opera Company so it could tour through many small towns across the United States.

entrance, and about the cramped doors leading inside. "The entrance to a great museum should welcome passersby, not rise above them like a wall," she said. A few weeks later, Lila donated the money to build a brand new entrance hall.

When the hall was completed in 1970, Lila was given a tour. She was impressed by its magnificent

Lila donated the money for a bright new entrance
hall to the Metropolitan Museum. Her gift included
the huge bouquets seen along the walls.

Lila enjoyed giving people an opportunity to learn about art and culture.

dome and polished marble floors. But Lila felt something was missing. She decided the museum was too cold, too big, and too unfriendly. She ordered huge bouquets of flowers to be placed along the walls. The hall burst into color. Lila gave enough money so that wilting flowers could quickly be replaced. Today, if you visit the Metropolitan Museum of Art, you can see Lila's gift blooming fresh every day.

DeWitt believed that young people should receive the best education possible.

Whenever the Wallaces supported a cause, they didn't talk about their generosity. They didn't want to draw attention to themselves. Over the years, they quietly contributed to hundreds of worthwhile causes. DeWitt died in 1981, and Lila died in 1984. But even after their deaths, the Wallaces' generosity continues to fund the dreams of thousands of people.

In Your Community

DeWitt and Lila Wallace established two funds to support the causes they believed in. These funds give out about $100 million a year. DeWitt's fund supports education in the United States. Lila's fund gives money to art programs.

Do you have a cause you believe in? You don't need a lot of money to

Timeline

Lila attends the School of Social Services at the University of Oregon.

DeWitt enlists in the army; Lila works to improve factory conditions.

DeWitt publishes the first edition of *Reader's Digest*.

DeWitt Wallace is born on November 12.

 1887 — 1889 — 1907 — 1909 — 1915 — 1917 — 1918 — 1920 — 1921 —

Lila Acheson is born on December 25.

Lila attends Ward-Belmont College in Nashville, Tennessee.

DeWitt publishes *Getting the Most Out of Farming*.

DeWitt is severely wounded in the war.

DeWitt and Lila are married on October 15.

help support it. What can you do to help your community? Pick something that interests or excites you, then try to make it happen. Do you like sports? Organize a league in your neighborhood. Do you like to read? Collect used books for the library. As the Wallaces proved, there are hundreds of ways to make your community a more beautiful and enjoyable place.

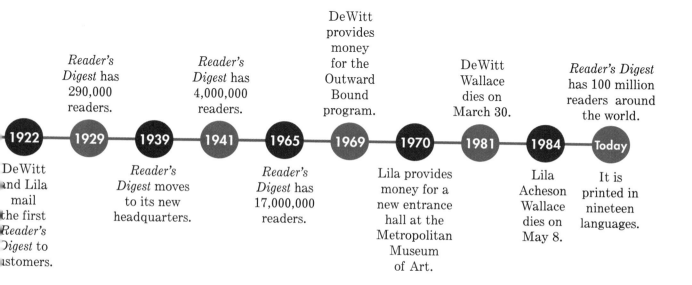

1922	1929	1939	1941	1965	1969	1970	1981	1984	Today
DeWitt and Lila mail the first *Reader's Digest* to customers.	*Reader's Digest* has 290,000 readers.	*Reader's Digest* moves to its new headquarters.	*Reader's Digest* has 4,000,000 readers.	*Reader's Digest* has 17,000,000 readers.	DeWitt provides money for the Outward Bound program.	Lila provides money for a new entrance hall at the Metropolitan Museum of Art.	DeWitt Wallace dies on March 30.	Lila Acheson Wallace dies on May 8.	*Reader's Digest* has 100 million readers around the world. It is printed in nineteen languages.

To Find Out More

Here are some additional resources to help you learn more about *Reader's Digest*, DeWitt and Lila Wallace, and causes they believed in:

Books

Crawford, Jean, ed. ***Art and Music.*** Time-Life Books, 1994.

Emmond, Kenneth. ***Manitoba.*** Children's Press, 1992.

Fradin, Dennis Brindell. ***Minnesota.*** Children's Press, 1994.

Fradin, Dennis Brindell. ***New York.*** Children's Press, 1993.

Kuller, Alison M. ***Outward Bound School.*** Troll, 1990.

Todd, Richard. ***Giving.*** Crosswalk, 1994.

Organizations and Online Sites

Reader's Digest Association
Reader's Digest Road
Pleasantville, NY 10570
http://www.readersdigest.com
On the homepage for *Reader's Digest*, you'll find plenty of information about *Reader's Digest* articles and products, including a variety of books for young readers.

DeWitt Wallace-Reader's Digest Fund
2 Park Avenue, 23rd Floor
New York, NY 10016
http://www.dewittwallace.org/
This is DeWitt Wallace's charity fund, which grants money to educational causes.

Lila Wallace-Reader's Digest Fund
2 Park Avenue, 23rd Floor
New York, NY 10016
http://www.lilawallace.org/
Facts and information about Lila's charity fund, which grants money to arts and music organizations.

Index

About the Author

B rendan January was born and raised in Pleasantville, New York, where he often walked through the Wallaces' former backyard on his way to school. He graduated from Pleasantville High School, and went on to earn a degree in History and English literature at Haverford College in Pennsylvania. Mr. January is the author of several other books for Children's Press.